Do I struggle with any of these topics?

☐ Building Relationships

☐ Communication

☐ Creating Healthy Boundaries

☐ Finances

☐ Health

☐ Lack of Motivation

☐ Low Self-Esteem

☐ Mental Health

☐ Other: _____

☐ Self-care Routine

☐ Self-Identity

☐ Spirituality

☐ Trauma

☐ Trust

☐ Understanding Myself

Date: Forever Mood

Dear Self,

It's time for me to release my thoughts and feelings that are suppressed. I will be open to fill my cup and replenish my mind, body, and soul. This is the beginning of my healing journey.

Sincerely,

I Owe It To Myself!

Resources

Name : _____

Phone : _____

Address : _____

Notes : _____

Name : _____

Phone : _____

Address : _____

Notes : _____

Name : _____

Phone : _____

Address : _____

Notes : _____

Name : _____

Phone : _____

Address : _____

Notes : _____

Resources

Name : _____

Phone : _____

Address : _____

Notes : _____

Name : _____

Phone : _____

Address : _____

Notes : _____

Name : _____

Phone : _____

Address : _____

Notes : _____

Name : _____

Phone : _____

Address : _____

Notes : _____

Resources

Name : _____

Phone : _____

Address : _____

Notes : _____

Name : _____

Phone : _____

Address : _____

Notes : _____

Name : _____

Phone : _____

Address : _____

Notes : _____

Name : _____

Phone : _____

Address : _____

Notes : _____

Resources

Name : _____

Phone : _____

Address : _____

Notes : _____

Name : _____

Phone : _____

Address : _____

Notes : _____

Name : _____

Phone : _____

Address : _____

Notes : _____

Name : _____

Phone : _____

Address : _____

Notes : _____

Self care IS NOT Selfish

- [ ] --
- [ ] --
- [ ] --
- [ ] --
- [ ] --
- [ ] --
- [ ] --

Notes

Self care IS NOT selfish

- [ ] --
- [ ] --
- [ ] --
- [ ] --
- [ ] --
- [ ] --
- [ ] --

Notes

Self care IS NOT selfish

☐ --
☐ --
☐ --
☐ --
☐ --
☐ --
☐ --

Notes

Self care IS NOT selfish

- [ ] --
- [ ] --
- [ ] --
- [ ] --
- [ ] --
- [ ] --
- [ ] --

Notes

Self care
IS NOT ←
selfish

- [ ] --
- [ ] --
- [ ] --
- [ ] --
- [ ] --
- [ ] --
- [ ] --

Notes

Dear Self,

I

Am

Proud

Of

You

Alainea is a self publisher from the DMV area. She is passionate about helping people embrace their strengths and achieve their goals.
Her motto is "It Starts With You".

Dear Self Journal allows you to release your feelings that are buried within. Fill your cup with the goal to restore, release, and carve the time for self-care. You owe it to yourself. It starts with you to take the first step in your healing journey.

Her previous published books include *Visionary Destiny* "handheld vision board" and *I Am* coloring and activity book. Alainea's mission is to help individuals who are willing to explore options of accountability, growth, and self-care.

Alainea Hilton
Author

Thank You!

Follow me for more:

Email: Vision@eye-see-hope.com

 Visionary Destiny   Visionary Destiny

 Visionary_Destiny

Made in the USA
Columbia, SC
22 May 2024

35606343R00111